To Mary Elizabeth

Christmas 2001

with love from

Sheila &

Chris

The Lion Book of First Prayers

For children who want to talk to God

The Lion Book of
First Prayers

Compiled by Su Box

Pictures by Leon Baxter

LION
Children's Books

Published by
Lion Publishing plc
Sandy Lane West, Oxford, England
www.lion-publishing.co.uk
ISBN 0 7459 3441 2
ISBN 0 7459 3944 9 (white gift edition)
ISBN 0 7459 3943 0 (red gift edition)
ISBN 0 7459 3945 7 (blue gift edition)

First hardback edition 1998
10 9 8 7 6 5

Acknowledgments
With thanks to the many children, parents and teachers
who helped with the creation of this book

A catalogue record for this book is available
from the British Library

Printed and bound in Malaysia

Contents

Introduction

The purpose of this book is to help young children take their first steps in prayer, so that talking to God becomes a natural everyday experience. These prayers are a starting-point – showing enjoyable and simple ways to give thanks and praise, to say sorry or to ask for God's help.

The prayers have been chosen to show that God is interested in every aspect of a child's life and that people can pray at any time and anywhere. Many of the prayers have been created by children themselves and show that you don't need special words to talk to God. In fact, talking to God can be just like talking to a loving parent or a best friend.

The book follows the pattern of a typical child's day, so you will find prayers to suit most moods and occasions. (A subject index offers additional direction to prayers on particular themes.)

You might like to ask your child to close their eyes and put their hands together as you read the words. Or they may prefer to look at the delightful pictures, which give added meaning to each prayer. Some of the prayers include suggestions for ways children can make a prayer their own (by saying the name of a friend or talking about a special experience), while others lend themselves to simple actions. And, of course, you can encourage children to join you in saying 'Amen' at the end of a prayer.

Before long, your child will have favourite prayers they want to return to again and again. But this book will also provide a first step towards a child's own prayers, helping him or her gain the confidence to share their own thoughts and feelings with God. This can be the first step of a lifelong friendship.

In the Morning

Waking Up

This morning, God,
This is your day.
I am your child,
Show me your way.
Amen

Thank you for each morning
I wake to a new day.
Thank you for my family,
For friends and fun and play.
Amen

You wake me up, Father, to a new day.
Thanks to you I'm living.
Help me to live today as you wish.

A child's prayer

Thank you for this sunny morning.
It makes me happy.
Amen

Me

Lord, you know all about me...
I praise you because you made me
in an amazing and wonderful way.

From Psalm 139

Father God,
You made me,
You love me,
You look after me.
Thank you, God.

Dear God, Mum says I'm special.
Is it true there's no one else just like me?

A child's question

Dear God,
You know all about me:
The good things
and the bad things.
But you still think I'm special.
Thank you, God.

Let my thoughts and words
please you, Lord.
Amen

Two little eyes to look to God
Two little ears to hear his word,
Two little feet to walk in his ways,
Two little lips to sing his praise,
Two little hands to do his will,
And one little heart to love him still.

(This makes a good action rhyme.)

God, I can run and jump
and shout and SING!
I can skip and clap
and stamp and SWING!
Thank you for making me!

Family Times

I love them
And they love me,
Thank you for
My family.

Dear God, we've got a new baby!
He's* little and cries a lot.
When he's bigger I can play with him.
Thanks, God, for my new brother.

* Change throughout to suit a girl if necessary.

I'm sorry, God. I love my sister,*
but sometimes we fight.

* Change to suit a brother if necessary.

My prayer. God is good.
He gives us friends and family.
Amen

A child's prayer

Thank you for my Gran and
her stories and cuddles.
Amen

Grandad takes me for walks.
He's very old. Please mend his bad knee.

Philip (aged 5)

Bless this house which is our home;
May we welcome all who come.

Meal Times

Each time we eat,
may we remember God's love.
Amen

A child's prayer

God is great;
God is good.
And we thank him
For our food.

For every cup and plateful
God make us truly grateful.

Thank you for the world so sweet,
Thank you for the food we eat.
Thank you for the birds that sing,
Thank you, God, for everything.

Dear God, thank you for all you give us.
Please help us to remember the needs
of others.
Amen

Through the Day

Playing

Loving Father, on this day
Make us happy in our play,
Kind and helpful, playing fair,
Letting others have a share.
Amen

It's playgroup* day today!
Thank you, God.

* Change to whatever is appropriate for your child.

Dear God,
Thank you for making everything.
When I make something I think of you.
Amen

Dear God,
Thank you for painting and for
all the lovely colours. I'm glad you
don't mind if I make a mess!
Amen

40

Dear Lord
Thank you for football
Thank you for the sea
Thank you for the world
And thank you for me.

Mark (aged 7)

Helping

Help me, God, to show how much I love
Mum and Dad by helping them.
Amen

Dear God, please look after me today
and help me to help others.
Amen

Dear God, I like to help, but I'm not always good at it. Please help me to get things right.
Amen

Thank you for the person who
helped me today.
Amen

My Friends

Thank you, God, for my friend.*
Please help me to be kind and share
my toys.

* Ask child to say the name of his or her friend.

Thank you for special friends
and games and secrets.
Amen.

Joseph (aged 5)

Dear God, I've been bad
And made my friend* sad.
Please help me to say sorry.

* Ask child to say the name of his or her friend.

Dear God, my friend* isn't well.
Please make him* feel better again.
Amen

* Ask child to say friend's name and substitute 'her' if necessary.

Thank you, God, for friends who care
when I'm feeling sad.
Thank you, God, for friends who share
and make me feel glad.

Jesus, you are my best friend.
Thank you for all the things
you give to me.
Amen

Days Out

Dear Lord on high,
Make a clear sky,
Make the day fine
And let the sweet sun shine.

Dear God,
It was fun in the park today.
Thank you for my friends and play.
Amen

For trees so tall
And flowers so small,
Thank you, God.
Amen

Hello, God, I like our world.
Thank you for making it.

Stephen (aged 4)

I'm sorry I was naughty at the
shops today.
Amen

A child's prayer

Dear God, thank you for cars, because
we can go a long way in them.

Gavin (aged 7)

Thank you for making the animals at the zoo and giving elephants big ears.
Amen

Ruth (aged 4)

Dear God, today we saw lots of wild animals! Please stop people who want to hurt them.
Amen

Weather

Thank you, God, for sunshine,
Thank you, God, for spring,
Thank you, God, for sending
Every lovely thing.

Dear God,
Please send lots of sun and showers
to help my seeds grow into flowers.
Amen

It's raining!
Rain makes our garden grow.
The ducks like rain.
Rain makes puddles I can jump in.
Thank you, God, for rain.

Thank you, God, for splashy puddles.
Amen

A child's prayer

Thank you, God, for making rainbows.
The lovely colours make me happy
on a wet day.

Amy (aged 5)

Dear God, please help me to remember
that you are bigger than the scary
thunder.
Amen

Thank you, God, for snowy days,
For those freezing, 'cold nose' days.
Amen

Thank you for the snowflakes,
Falling soft and white,
Making everything I see
Look clean and bright.

Animals

Thank you for the little ladybird
that sat on my finger today.
Amen

A child's prayer

Dear Father, hear and bless
Your beasts and singing birds,
And guard with tenderness
Small things that have no words.

Dear God, can I tell you a secret?
I've got a new pet!*
Amen

A child's prayer

* Ask child to describe this new pet.

Dear God,
Thank you for my pets.* Please help
me to look after them and make them
feel loved.
Amen

* Ask child to name any family pets.

I like little puppies and kittens.
But why do they have to get big?
Amen

Luke (aged 5)

Father God, my pet* has died.
I miss him so much. Please help me
to be happy again.
Amen

*Ask child to say pet's name.

Thank you for the cows that give us milk.

A child's prayer

Dear God, thank you for tadpoles.
I can't believe tadpoles turn into frogs.

Stephen (aged 3)

Dear God, thank you for giving the whale the big sea to swim in.

James (aged 5)

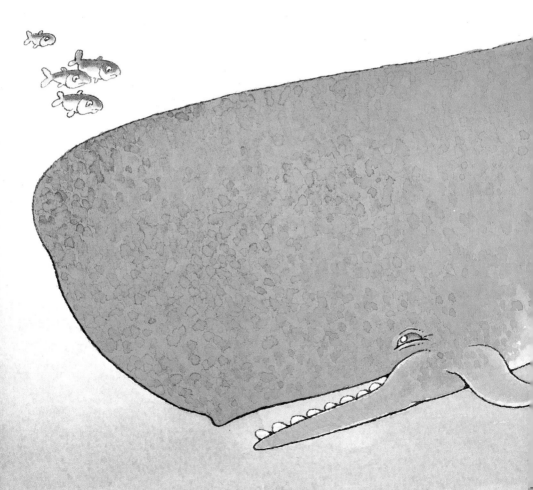

Happy Times

Today we're going to the seaside!
Thank you, God, that I can paddle in
the sea and play in the rock pools.
Amen

Thank you for summer:
For paddling and picnics
and holidays and ices.
It's fun in the sun!
Thanks God.

My lost teddy is back again.
Thank you, God.

Susie (aged 3)

Thank you for my Mum and Dad
and all the fun* we have together.
Amen

* Ask child to name experiences they have enjoyed.

Thank you, God,
for special days to look forward to
and special days to remember.
Amen

Thanks, God, for our holiday and all the
happy times we had.
Amen

Dear God, I just feel good knowing that
you are everywhere. That's all.

A child's prayer

I love you
my God!
I love you more than anything
in the world!
Praise to you, God.

Sad Times

I was sad today, God.
Thank you for being with me.
Amen

Thank you, God, for loving me,
even when I am cross.
Amen

Dear God, I am ill.
Thank you for the people
looking after me.
Please make me better.
Amen.

Dear God, please help my friend* be
happy when their mum or dad can't
be around.
Amen

* Ask child to name any friend they know in this situation.

I'm lonely, God.
Please help me to feel happy again.
Amen

My Gran* has died.
I won't see her any more.
Mum says she's living with you now.
Please look after her.

* Substitute name as appropriate.

Dear God, knowing you are with me
when I'm sad is like knowing that the sun
is only hidden behind the clouds.
Amen

At Night

Quiet Times

Thank you for time
for a cuddle and a hug,
a time to share secrets
and feel safe and snug.
Amen

Thank you, God, for ears to hear.
When I'm quiet I can hear all sorts
of noises.*

* Ask child to listen and share what he or she can hear.

Thank you for the Bible. I like to hear stories about my friend Jesus.
Amen

Dear God, please help me to be quiet,
so that I can listen to you.
Amen

Bath Time

Thank you, God, for water
So that I can splash –
Having lots of bath-time fun
As I wash.

Two eyes, two ears,
One mouth, one nose;
Fingers, tummy,
Knees and toes.
You made all these –
Thanks, God, for making me!

Bedtime

I go to bed and sleep in peace,
for you, Lord, keep me safe.

From Psalm 4

Bless my eyes
And bless my head,
Bless my dreams
Upon this bed.

Dear God, I like the twinkling stars.
But how do you keep them up?

A child's question

I see the moon
And the moon sees me.
God bless the moon,
And God bless me.

Dear God,
I'm sorry I was naughty today.
Please help me to be nice to Mum and
Dad tomorrow.
Amen

A child's prayer

Now that I lie down to sleep,
I ask you, Lord, your child to keep;
Your love be with me all the night,
And wake me with the morning light.

Dear God, when I wake up in the night and feel afraid, please help me to remember you are close beside me. Amen

Special Days and Prayers

Birthdays

Today is my birthday, God!
Thank you for today and every day.

It's my birthday today.
Now I'm a year older,
help me to grow bigger
in a way that pleases you.
Amen

Dear Jesus, it's my birthday
and I am four* today.
Thank you for all the lovely things*
that make this a special day.
Amen

* Ask child to say their age and what makes today special for them.

Sunday

This is the day that the Lord has made.
Let us rejoice and be glad today!

From Psalm 118

Dear God,
I like it when we go to church,
We sing and then we pray.
We hear some Bible stories
And meet our friends and play.
Amen

Thank you for church and singing
and all my friends there.
Amen

A child's prayer

God, Sunday is your special day,
and I like it because Mum and Dad
don't make me 'hurry up'.

James (aged 5)

Christmas

Father God, thank you for giving us your
son baby Jesus.
Amen

A child's prayer

116

Dear God,
Thank you for showing your love
by giving us the baby Jesus.
Help us to share Christmas love
everywhere.

Jesus, did you know we have party
on your birthday?
It's because you were a special baby.
Can you come one year?

Daniel (aged 4)

Thank you, God, for Christmas surprises
And presents of all shapes and sizes.
For family and friends, and everyone
Who makes our Christmas Day such fun.
For special food and games to play
As we enjoy Jesus' birthday.

Easter

Thank you, God, that you love us
so much that you sent Jesus to die for us
so that we can be friends with you.
Amen

When Jesus died his friends were sad.
When Jesus rose his friends were glad.
I am happy too this Easter morning.

Dear Jesus, thank you for the new life
that Easter brings.
Amen

Dear Jesus, it hurt you on the cross.
But you got better, and you made
EVERYTHING better again.

Evie (aged 3)

The Lord's Prayer

(paraphrased for children)*

Our Father God,
We want you to be our King for ever:
then everyone will live as you want.
Give us each day all that we need.
Forgive us for the wrong things we do,
as we forgive people who hurt us.
Help us stop wanting to do bad things.
And keep us from all harm.
Amen

* Jesus loved to talk to God and pray. He taught his friends the
special prayer which we call 'The Lord's Prayer'.

Subject Index

Acknowledgments

Thanks go to all those who have given permission to include material in this book, as indicated in the list below. Every effort has been made to trace and contact copyright owners. We apologize for any inadvertent omissions or errors. All prayers except those acknowledged in the main text or listed below have been written by the author.

Pages 12 and 58: From *Children in Conversation with God*. Copyright © The Lutheran World Federation. Reproduced by kind permission of The Lutheran World Federation.

Pages 13, 25 and 36: From *The Infant Teacher's Prayer Book*, edited by Dorothy M. Prescott. Copyright © 1964 Blandford Press. Used by permission of Cassell plc.

Page 15: From *Prayers to Use with Under Fives* by Mary Bacon and Jean Hodgson. Published by the National Christian Education Council.

Page 19: By Colin C. Kerr, copyright © Mrs B. Kerr, from *CSSM Choruses, Book 1*.

Page 20: From *The Children's Book of Prayers*, compiled by Louise Carpenter. Copyright © 1988 Blackie and Sons Ltd.

Page 22: From *Talking to God* by Margaret Barfield. Copyright © 1997 Margaret Barfield. Published by Scripture Union.

Page 31: Copyright © 1959 and 1987 by Concordia Publishing House. Used with permission.

Pages 32, 52, 69, 85, 103 and 105 are all traditional prayers.

Page 33: From *Hymns and Songs for Children*. National Society.

Page 41: From *The Lion Prayer Collection*, compiled by Mary Batchelor. Copyright © 1992 Mary Batchelor. Published by Lion Publishing plc.

Pages 57 and 76: From *Children at Prayer*, edited by Rachel Stowe. Copyright © 1996 HarperCollins Publishers. Published by Marshall Pickering.

Page 60: From *My Own Book of Prayers*, compiled by Mary Batchelor. Copyright © 1984 Lion Publishing.

Pages 86 and 108: From *My First Prayer Book*. Copyright © Gwen Tansey and Cathy Jenkins. Used with permission of the publishers, HarperCollins Religious (Melbourne).

Page 99: Based on *Hello, Baby* by Felicity Henderson. Copyright © 1995 Lion Publishing.

Page 101: From *The Day I Fell Down the Toilet* by Steve Turner. Copyright © 1996 Steve Turner. Published by Lion Publishing plc.